How to Help

**A guide to helping someone manage
mental distress**

TIM WATKINS
For
LIFE SURFING

ISBN-13: 978-1492392873
ISBN-10: 1492392871

CONTENTS

Life Surfing

Why Help?

Although there remains widespread stigma around mental illness, this is not the reason why most people hold back from offering help. We do not readily help those affected by mental illness because of our own ignorance and the fear that we might do the wrong thing. The result is that we stand aside and do nothing, unaware that doing nothing is the worst thing we can do.

Someone who is struggling to come to terms with mental distress will be bewildered, not understanding what is happening to them and desperate for answers. Seeing those close to them—family, friends, colleagues and neighbours—apparently rejecting them and abandoning them to their fate simply adds to the psychological trauma of a condition that is going to take time and support to overcome.

Most people with mental health problems do not go on to develop mental illness. Of those who do, the majority experience relatively short episodes.

Recovery can be rapid and sustained. But recovery is hindered by a lack of support, of treatment and of self-help.

So long as those affected by mental illness are prepared to work toward recovery, and provided those around them offer appropriate support and encouragement, there is no reason why they cannot go on to lead full, productive and meaningful lives in future.

This guide will introduce you to the things you can do to support someone you care about to manage and overcome their mental health problems.

Mental Illness

Mental health problems are common, affecting between 25 and 30 percent of us in any year. Mental illness is less common. Around 23 percent will visit their GP to discuss their mental health problems, but only 10 percent will be diagnosed with a mental illness. Of these, three-quarters will be treated solely by their GP. Less than one percent of us will require in-patient treatment.

The majority of mental health problems are 'reactive' - they are a response to stressful life events and situations that involve our feeling trapped or our having to come to terms with loss or change. These can include such things as bereavement, caring, debt, disability, moving home, over-working, relationship breakdown and unemployment.

In most cases, people who experience mental health problems in relation to events like these are able to recover reasonably quickly once the event has been resolved. Recovery can be hastened with appropriate support and self-help.

In some cases, a person's mental health deteriorates and they develop a common mental illness such as anxiety or depression. In most cases, these are 'reactive'. However, a small minority of those affected have 'endogenous' (i.e., from within) illness that cannot be explained as a reaction to external factors.

Although most common mental illnesses are self-healing (given time, most people recover), around a fifth of those affected develop severe and enduring mental illness that can become life-threatening. Since there is no way of knowing who is who in advance, it is important that anyone with a mental illness seeks medical advice and support.

Getting medical help is also important because a small proportion of cases of mental illness are the result of underlying physical disease such as diabetes, liver disease and thyroid problems.

A minority (about three percent of us) develop severe mental illness, mainly bipolar disorder or schizophrenia. These usually develop from mid-teens through to early twenties, and are more common in males than females.

Although people with severe mental illness are much more likely to need intensive medical support, including stays in hospital, the prognosis for this group is good. Around a third will be able to get on with their lives without further medical support, and will never have another episode. A third will be able to get on with their lives with minimal medical support (usually staying on medication to stabilise their condition).

Medicine v self-help?

Given the fear and stigma surrounding mental illness, it is no surprise that many of those affected look to self-help as an alternative to medicine.

In the case of relatively minor mental health problems, this is not unreasonable. Avoiding diagnosis means avoiding the stigma of having "mental illness" recorded on your health records and, as a consequence, putting future employment and access to financial services in jeopardy.

However, there is a very real risk that without help a 'problem' will rapidly deteriorate and become a serious illness. If this happens, then it will be impossible to avoid the "mental illness" label anyway.

A better approach is to use both self-help and medicine according to whether they help or hinder recovery.

A good clinician will tell you that medication and talking therapies such as cognitive behavioural therapy (CBT) are effective treatments for mental illness. An honest clinician will also tell you that medication is only effective in about 70 percent of cases, and CBT is only effective in 50 percent of cases. They may also add that in perhaps 10 percent of cases, side-effects and problems with the therapy can make matters worse.

Unfortunately, there is no way of knowing in advance what will or will not work. Finding the right treatment is often a matter of trial and error.

The same is true for self-help. We can all make health-promoting changes to our lives. Some will greatly improve our wellbeing, some will have little effect, some may even leave us feeling worse off. Again, it is a matter of trial and error.

Eventually, the correct balance of medical support and self-help will be found, and recovery will follow.

Support and motivation

Because each person affected by mental health problems and mental illness must find their own road to recovery, there will often be times when they just feel like giving up. Expressing sentiments like:

"I've tried that… it doesn't work"
"Well how is that going to help?"

This is where your help and support can be invaluable. You can provide the listening ear, the shoulder to cry on, and the caring encouragement that will be needed to nudge them along the road to recovery.

How to Help

It is helpful to understand the components of mental health (or 'wellbeing'). The model we use is of someone pushing a burden along a slope:

- o The burden (is it light or heavy?) is about how we are as individuals. It includes our skills and abilities, our beliefs and thoughts, our emotions, our physical bodies, and the way we interact socially.
- o The traction of the slope (is it firm or slippery?) represents the various institutions within which we live our lives. These include our families, neighbourhoods, workplaces, schools and colleges, clubs and associations, etc.

- o The angle of the slope (is it steep or shallow?) is about the wider environmental, political and economic conditions within which we live.

In the best scenario, someone will enjoy positive mental, emotional and physical health, will be utilising their skills and abilities and fully engaging with the world around them (their burden is light). Their institutions will be nurturing and enabling (the slope is firm). The environment, economic and political climate will be benign (the angle of the slope is shallow).

Notice that none of these things is entirely within anyone's control. Even when we act collectively through a popular democratic government, we cannot affect the environment or the global economy. Bringing about change to the institutions in our lives involves acting collectively, and in many cases requires professional support from advisers, advocates or lawyers.

We can, of course, work on ourselves. But even here, there are things that will be beyond our control. Much of our physical make up is down to the genes we inherit from our parents. These affect everything from the illness we might eventually die from to our cholesterol levels and blood pressure, through our height, arm and finger length, to our ability to hear music or to appreciate art.

When helping, encouraging and supporting someone who has mental health problems, we need to be aware of their limitations and look for constructive solutions that play to that person's strengths and abilities.

If, for example, someone has anxiety problems because they are under a lot of pressure at work, helping them manage the symptoms of anxiety will not be a sufficient response. The workplace pressure must also be addressed. This will require the help of other people. It might be as straightforward as encouraging them to talk to their line manager or it might mean involving occupational health, a trade union or even an employment lawyer.

Similarly, if someone has become depressed because they were made redundant, while encouraging them to manage the symptoms of depression will help, they will also need to get support to restructure their finances, claim any benefits or insurance payments they are entitled to, and get back into employment or training as quickly as possible.

Part of the support you can give will be to help them disentangle those things they can do for themselves, those things that they will need help with, and those things that are beyond their influence. You can then encourage them to do things for themselves and to seek the additional help they need.

Life Surfing

L.A.S.S.

The mnemonic 'LASS' provides a four-step model for helping someone who is experiencing a mental health problem or mental illness. Learning these steps will help you in any situation, whether you are dealing with a close relative or a complete stranger, and whether they have a relatively minor mental health problem or a severe mental illness.

LASS stands for:

- Listen (without judgement)
- Assess (and if necessary ask about suicide)
- Signpost to appropriate Support
- Encourage Self-help

Listen

For someone experiencing mental distress, being able to give voice to what they are experiencing and—crucially—knowing that they are heard is an important step on the road to recovery.

So, listening to someone who is experiencing mental distress is the starting point for helping.

Listening is a skill that has to be learned. You may think that you listen to people when you are having a conversation. However, if you focus on what is happening to you during a conversation, you will find that you are not listening for a considerable part of the time when the other person is speaking. You will find that as they are speaking:

- You are thinking about what you will say next
- You are distracted by thoughts about things you were doing or things you have to do later
- You become emotionally aroused in response to things they are saying (e.g., you might feel irritation, anger, concern, happiness, jealousy, etc)
- Your body's physical sensations interrupt your chain of thought (e.g., you might notice an itch, or feel discomfort in your legs or arms)
- Your mind drifts off onto other things.

Consciously focusing on what someone else is saying, without allowing these mental, emotional and physical processes to interfere is actually quite difficult. It is helpful to consciously adopt a "listening mode" when you are helping someone who is experiencing mental distress. Try to:

1. Bring your attention to your body—focus on feeling your feet on the floor, then focus up through your body, on your legs, hips, back, tummy, chest, hands, arms, shoulders, neck, head, face and scalp
2. Make sure you are breathing deeply and slowly
3. Say to yourself, "I am focusing on listening now".

You should find that this helps you to be present, and to be less distracted by the things that you had been doing or by thoughts about what you are going to do later.

Listening Skills:

Stop Talking
Don't interrupt
Show interest
Concentrate
Ask questions
Positive body language

Remember that the aim of this type of listening is to encourage the person you are with to open up, and to allow them to talk about their distress. As such, you do not want to respond to what they are saying as you would if you were having a conversation. Rather, you should encourage them to keep talking.

For example:

o Respond in an open-ended manner. Use phrases like, "that sounds very painful" or "I can hear that you are in a great deal of distress"

o Respond with questions such as, "That sounds very difficult, can you tell me more?" or "How does that make you feel?"

- o Use body language to show that you are open, and want to know more. Gently nodding and moving your hand can also signal that you want them to keep talking.

It is important that you learn to suspend judgement when you are helping someone who is experiencing mental distress.

Remember that a key aspect of mental health problems is that they are not rational. As such, it is very likely that someone affected by mental illness will say things that you simply cannot understand or do not believe. What they say may even make you feel angry or upset. Nevertheless, what they are telling you is true for them.

Being non-judgemental means not responding to what someone is saying by:

- o Displaying your emotions through your body language
- o Answering back
- o Arguing
- o Contradicting
- o Allowing your posture to close.

This is easier said than done, as you need to be focused on consciously listening if you are to avoid giving away your thoughts and feelings through your body language or through a spontaneous quip before you have had time to check yourself.

This does not, of course, mean that you have to collude with what they are saying. Nor should you allow them to act on false beliefs if this might cause them harm.

Many people with mental illness will receive talking (psychological) therapies that will help them overcome unrealistic thoughts and beliefs. However, this is a skilled intervention that needs to be delivered carefully. Simply telling them they are wrong is not going to work, and will most likely result in their no longer wanting to talk about their problems with you.

Assess

In assessing what is happening for the person you are helping, it is useful to understand some of the warning signs that can indicate someone has a mental health problem. (We have set out the symptoms of the various mental illnesses that you may encounter in our guides to *Anxiety* and *Depression*, and in the book *Helping Hands*).

While many of the symptoms of mental illness are invisible, and known only to the person experiencing them, it is possible to observe that something is wrong by looking out for:

- o "Quick fix" substances and behaviours
- o Changes in appearance
- o Loss of performance at work and at home
- o Social withdrawal.

Almost all of us reach for "quick fix" substances such as alcohol, caffeine, chocolate, nicotine and sugar when we are stressed. Each of these substances make you feel better in the short-term. If, for example, you are someone who has a glass of wine to help you unwind after a stressful day at work, you are likely to turn to wine in larger quantities if you suffer severe or enduring stress. The effects of this will become apparent to people around you.

Some people also turn to behaviours like "being busy" (expending a lot of effort but not getting much done), comfort eating, taking risks and casual sex. These may also be apparent to people around them.

Over time, some of the effects of mental health problems can become visible. For example, some people may lose their appetite, resulting in their losing weight. Others might neglect their personal appearance. These changes will become obvious to people around them.

Mental illness also impacts on someone's ability to perform tasks both at work and at home. This can be the result of symptoms like impaired concentration, memory loss and problems with motor function. Mental illness is also accompanied by physical exhaustion, making it very difficult to complete tasks.

Unfortunately, while a drop in performance is very obvious, the underlying mental health problem is not.

This often results in people being disciplined at work and having relationship problems at home.

Finally, people experiencing mental health problems often struggle in social situations. This can result in their finding excuses to withdraw. This is a particular problem for those who are not in employment, as this makes it much easier to avoid going out. While withdrawing may appear beneficial (for example, allowing for rest and recuperation) it is counter-productive in the longer-term, and may result in full-blown agoraphobia.

In assessing what is happening, it is important to look out for these changes in behaviour and appearance. This is particularly true where you are able to relate these changes to stressful life events and situations such as bereavement, caring for others, debt, divorce or separation, illness, redundancy, etc.

You should be particularly concerned where the impact on the person is so great that they are no longer able to get on with their normal daily activities.

So, for example, if you notice that your next door neighbour has been increasingly withdrawn since his wife died six months ago, and you are concerned that he has lost weight and does not appear to be looking after himself, he might have become depressed. And while this might resolve itself without help, it may not. It might be worth encouraging him to get help.

Ask About Suicide

Although suicide is very rare, more people kill themselves than die in road accidents every year. Suicide is also the biggest killer of young women and the second biggest killer of young men. Because mental illness is a causal factor in most suicides, it is important that you take seriously any indication that someone may be considering taking their own life.

Do:

- ✓ Ask about suicide (try to be direct)
- ✓ Try to reduce the risk
- ✓ Encourage them to talk
- ✓ Show that you are prepared to listen without judging
- ✓ Tell them you care and are willing to help
- ✓ Focus on getting them through the immediate crisis rather than worrying about the long-term
- ✓ Agree to reasonable requests
- ✓ Ask if there is someone they would like to speak to (e.g., a friend, family member, medical practitioner or support worker).

Don't:

- ✗ Express shock
- ✗ Judge, criticise or blame
- ✗ Dare them to do it
- ✗ Talk about the sanctity of life
- ✗ Use guilt to try to dissuade them

    ✘   Leave them until you are sure the crisis has passed or appropriate support has arrived

    ✘   Be bound to secrecy.

Signpost to Appropriate Support

There is a range of potential help available to someone experiencing mental distress. Formal support includes:

- Charities and voluntary groups
- Employment support agencies
- General Practice
- Specialist Community Mental Health Teams (CMHTs)
- Private mental health services.

The support available will vary depending on where you live. For example, many charities run patient-led self-management groups. Others run voluntary counselling services. However, because these services are run by volunteers, they are not available throughout the country. Moreover, some services can have long waiting lists, particularly in areas where formal NHS services are in short supply.

General Practice is usually the first point of contact for NHS services. Initial assessment will either be by a doctor or (in some parts of the country) a "gateway worker". If a mental illness is diagnosed, they may be able to offer treatment and support within the practice.

This might include:

- ○ Medication
- ○ Counselling
- ○ Computerised talking therapies
- ○ Books on prescription
- ○ Exercise on prescription
- ○ Expert Patient Programme training.

In most cases, mental illness is treated entirely within general practice. However, where a condition is severe or treatment-resistant, or where there may be a risk of suicide, the doctor will make a referral to a CMHT. This is a specialist team made up of people from across several disciplines including psychiatry, psychology, mental health nursing, occupational therapy, physiotherapy and social work. The CMHT can offer a targeted package of care using treatments and support that are not available in General Practice.

NHS services are in short supply in many areas of the UK. This means that even when someone's need is recognised, they may not be able to secure appropriate treatment and support for several months. For this reason, it is worth considering what alternative provision might be available.

In some areas, employment agencies like Job Centre Plus can provide access to Cognitive Behavioural Therapy more readily than general practice. So where someone is currently unemployed or incapacitated and their mental illness is a factor, this avenue is worth exploring.

If someone is in work, their employer may offer psychological support either directly or through an "Employee Assistance Programme". Again, access to support through an employer is usually much quicker than through the NHS.

If they are a member of a scheme like BUPA, or if they have a medical insurance policy, they may find that they are entitled to private psychological support. Alternatively, they may also want to think about paying for private support themselves if they have the means to do so (but be aware that this can run to several thousand pounds). Unlike the NHS, there is no waiting list for private mental health services.

Encourage Self-Help

Self-help is the final element of our LASS mnemonic. For many people it is the most important. This is because most mental illness is self-healing. That is, given time, and assuming the stressors that triggered the episode have been removed, most people recover.

Unfortunately, because each of us is different, there is no instant model or recipe for recovery. As with medicine, there is only a process of trial and error. Seen in this way, the main issue in dealing with mental illness is to understand:

- The things that promote recovery, and
- The things that hinder recovery.

There are, however, some broad areas that you can encourage the person you are helping to address. These are:

- Social engagement
- Physical health
- Emotional health
- Thoughts and beliefs
- Core skills and abilities.

Social engagement

Remember that social withdrawal is a key symptom of most mental illnesses. However, giving in to withdrawal leads to a downward spiral in which the thought of re-engaging appears ever more daunting.

It is important to start where the person is with this, not where you would like them to be. For example, if someone has become so anxious about leaving the house that they experience a sense of panic just opening the front door, you will only make things worse if you take them to a busy shopping centre.

If they can only open the front door, start with that. Get them to stand in the open doorway until the panic subsides. Then try going out into the garden or street immediately outside. Then build up to walking along the street, then going a little further. One step at a time.

Your role is to keep encouraging them to take the next step.

Eventually even the most anxious person can be helped to return to normal social engagement in employment, family life and recreation. But only if they are prepared to take the necessary steps.

Physical health

Often, people with mental health problems will seek quick-fixes to help them deal with the negative feelings that are part of their illness. While quick fixes can help alleviate some of the symptoms in the short term, they make matters worse later on. For example, many people have an alcoholic drink to help unwind at the end of a stressful day. However, if you are having a lot of drinks every day, you will soon feel the negative health consequences.

Finding healthier alternatives to these quick fixes is an important part of self-help. The three key alternatives are:

- o Physical activity
- o Diet
- o Relaxation and sleep hygiene.

Exercise has been demonstrated to improve depression and anxiety, and can contribute to recovery for people with severe mental illnesses. We have used the term 'physical activity' rather than exercise because any physical activity (e.g., washing the car, doing housework or gardening) counts as exercise. Ideally, if they can do something outdoors, so they get plenty of daylight and fresh air, this will provide an additional boost.

Nor does physical activity have to be expensive. If they have the resources, they can join a health club or buy expensive equipment. However, they may just want to take a regular walk or jog every day. Alternatively, using a local swimming pool or leisure centre is not going to break the bank.

In some parts of the country, the NHS offers a free 'exercise on prescription' scheme. If they are eligible, they can work with a fitness coach at the local leisure centre for six to ten weeks to develop a personal fitness programme.

Encouraging healthy eating is also helpful. This is because too much unhealthy food will leave them feeling down, will cause them to become overweight, and will eventually result in a range of illnesses and health problems.

Although there are several vitamins and minerals that are thought to boost mood, it is more important that they eat a balanced and varied diet containing plenty of fruit and vegetables and just small amounts of fats, salt and sugar. It is also important to keep an eye on portion sizes.

If they need help losing weight, they may want to speak to an NHS dietician. They might also want to join a local Weight Watchers or Slimming World group (in some parts of the country, these are available through the NHS).

Addressing sleep problems and learning to relax is important to recovering from mental illness. In most cases, sleep becomes disrupted in three ways:

- o Inability to get to sleep at night. This is usually caused by a combination of stress and anxiety resulting in the body remaining alert when the mind is tired
- o Early waking. This is a result of the mind becoming alert during sleep, and is often accompanied by increased vivid dreaming. Eventually the mind wakes up even though the body is still tired.
- o Daytime sleeping is the consequence of the exhaustion that follows disrupted sleep at night. People become so tired that they try to "catch up" on the sleep they didn't get during the night. Unfortunately, this practice makes it harder to get to sleep in future, and can result in a vicious circle of being awake through the night and asleep during the day.

Sleep hygiene is a book in itself. However, some of the things that improve sleep include:

- Go to bed at the same time every night
- Keep the bedroom uncluttered, well ventilated, fragrant and not too hot or cold
- Only use the bedroom for sleep
- Make sure it is quiet and dark enough for sleep
- Have a warm milky drink and a biscuit before bed
- Have a warm bath
- Do some exercise earlier in the evening (but avoid anything strenuous immediately before bed)
- Read for 30-60 minutes before lights out
- Don't have a TV or computer in the bedroom
- Don't have a clock in the room (if you need an alarm clock, put it out of reach and out of sight).

Learning to relax can help with sleep problems and is an effective way of dealing with the stress and anxiety that often accompanies mental health problems.

Relaxation is more than just sitting on the couch watching TV or having a glass of wine with friends. It is about allowing your mind to slow down and letting your body really rest.

True relaxation requires practice –the fact that it doesn't happen straight away is often a source of frustration and can cause people to give up. It is important that you encourage perseverance.

The starting point for learning to relax is to set a regular time aside. This need only be 10-20 minutes. However, it is important that this time is protected so that relaxation won't be interrupted.

It is also helpful to find a comfortable space to use for relaxation. Ideally, this should be uncluttered, not too warm or cold, and well ventilated.

Each of us has to find out for ourselves whether we prefer to sit or lie down, and whether we are going to use the floor or whether we will use a chair or bed. All that matters is to find what is most comfortable and stick to it.

Some people are able to relax without any additional aid, just by tensing and un-tensing their muscles, and letting their mind empty. Others will use a relaxation CD (this might involve a spoken relaxation or it might just be relaxing sounds and music). Bio-feedback relaxation machines can be particularly effective relaxation aids, but they can also be very expensive.

Many people use complementary therapies such as aromatherapy, massage and reflexology to help them relax.

Some participate in gentle exercise such as tai chi and yoga, which also promote relaxation.

Emotional health

One of the difficulties with viewing stress, anxiety and depression as illness is that we tend to forget that they are often an entirely normal human response to difficult life events.

There comes a point where all of us (faced with enough stress for long enough) need to withdraw in order to lick our wounds and repair our lives. Unfortunately, a by-product of this withdrawal is to turn feelings in upon yourself.

The mental distress that we are trying to help with can often be as much to do with the turning in of emotions like anger, sadness, desolation and hate, as to do with external stressors. This is why two people can go through almost identical circumstances with totally different outcomes.

For someone experiencing mental distress, the simplest thing to do is to talk. By listening to them, we can help them get in touch with what they are feeling, and to give voice to their emotions.

For some people, talking may be enough. For others, it can be helpful to encourage them to engage in other healthy means of expressing their emotions, such as:

- Keeping a diary
- Writing poetry
- Art and crafts
- Playing or writing music

Activities like these provide a healthy and socially acceptable means of giving voice to feelings as an alternative to turning them in upon oneself or (worse still) becoming angry, or hurtful to other people.

Thoughts and beliefs

Understanding the distorted thoughts that characterise mental illness is really the preserve of clinical psychologists. However, being aware that someone with a mental illness may firmly believe something that isn't true is important.

Most often, people with mental health problems will become increasingly negative about themselves, people they know, and the world around them.

You can help someone who is experiencing negative and unrealistic thoughts by helping them to look at their thoughts more objectively.

You might encourage them to write down any troubling thoughts they have, and then look at the evidence to support the thought. Ask whether it is realistic or likely to be true.

Core skills and abilities

Each of us has personal abilities and skills that, when harnessed, help give meaning to our lives. However, we often find that life thwarts us, leaving us in roles where we are obliged to do things that we are not good at or that we do not enjoy doing.

In practice, you can either exercise your core skills and abilities in your work or (much more commonly) you can use work as a means of funding you so that you can deploy your skills and abilities through hobbies and/or through voluntary work.

In the long-term, someone experiencing mental distress may want to think about whether they are in the right employment. A change of employment might be possible, or they may be able to re-train or go back into education in order to develop their skills and abilities and to obtain the qualifications required to make the change.

In the short-term, you can encourage them to stay engaged in activities, hobbies or volunteering roles that allow them to use and develop their core skills and abilities.

This will be particularly important if they are not in employment. Mental distress is usually accompanied by extreme tiredness coupled to a tendency to withdraw from society. When someone feels this low, it may feel comfortable to stay at home catching up on sleep or trying to relax in front of the TV. But this can quickly become a vicious downward spiral—the less they engage and the more they sleep during the day, the worse their mental distress becomes.

Re-engaging with things they are good at, that they used to enjoy doing, or that they had always wanted to try, can form a key part of getting them out of this downward spiral and back into social circulation. Also, engaging in activities that utilise their core skills and abilities will help them to overcome feelings of low self-esteem and self-worth—particularly if they are able to use these in a voluntary role that allows them to help and support other people.

Life Surfing

Bringing it Together

Personal wellbeing is about bringing all of the elements of our lives into harmony.

When someone is socially engaged, physically fit, emotionally balanced, thinking rationally, and utilising their core skills and abilities, they will begin to experience a state that sportspeople refer to as "being in the zone" or that psychologists call "flow".

Of course, there are many external factors in life that can stand in the way of this. Climate change and global recession are beyond any one person's control, but impinge on everyone's life. Closer to home, things as diverse as the rate of crime or the availability of public transport in the area where you live will have an impact on wellbeing, as will social relations in work, among friends and within your family.

Recovery from mental health problems may not necessarily mean getting "in the zone", but it does mean improving personal resilience and taking steps to address those wider societal issues that can be affected.

Remember that this will be a process that takes time. So encourage the person you are helping to:

- o   Plan ahead
- o   Take small steps
- o   Keep a diary.

Without planning, it is easy to try to do too much or to overlook some of the things you will need to do to succeed. It is a bit like setting out to run a marathon without putting in the training and without buying appropriate footwear.

Closely allied to planning is breaking things down into small steps. This is particularly important for someone with mental health problems as their ability to perform will be impaired by their condition. As a result, they may plan in terms of what they could have done before they had problems rather than what they can realistically achieve now.

The aim is always to encourage them to make small improvements each time, but never to push them so far that they become exhausted and fail (this will set their recovery back).

Keeping a diary or record chart (you can download a free chart from www.depressiononline.org) is a useful means of measuring the effect of the things they are doing. For example, if they want to improve their mood or energy levels, they might give these a score from 1 to 10 for each day. Then they might measure a combination of the quick fixes they use (e.g., how much alcohol they consume) the formal help they are getting (e.g., antidepressants) and the various self-help approaches they are trying (e.g., going for a walk every day).

Over time they will find that some things make their mood and energy levels worse, some make no difference, and some make things better. This will help them to choose to avoid things that make them feel worse, and do more of the things that make them feel better.

Life Surfing

Look after yourself

Helping someone who has mental health problems can be a wearing process, particularly if your relationship to them means that you are going to be in for the long-term.

It is all too easy to let their needs take priority over yours. This opens you to the risk of prolonged stress and burn-out. Remember that if you get ill, you will not be able to help anyway. So set some boundaries and stick to them. And remember:

- o You can't do their recovery for them
- o Don't let them "test" your commitment by doing things to push you away
- o Keep an eye on your own stress levels
- o Take time out for yourself

- o Learn to relax (see above).

Self-help approaches are not just for people who have mental health problems. So if you are feeling stressed from helping them, you may want to consider doing something for yourself. You might engage in some physical activity, go to a yoga class or try a complementary therapy.

Remember to talk about any stress that you have from helping. Ideally, talk to a friend or relative (obviously, someone other than the person you are helping).

Failing this, take advantage of one of the many mental health helplines.

Finally, don't be afraid to ask for help. There are many public and third sector organisations aimed at people who support others.

About Life Surfing

Life Surfing is a not-for-profit Community Interest Company that was established to provide a coaching, mentoring and training approach for people experiencing common life problems that can cause stress, anxiety and depression.

Our mission is to help people learn to cope with life without the need to call on over-stretched NHS services that are better deployed to help people with severe mental illness.

Over the years we have found that there is a huge amount that people can do to develop their personal resources and to foster their own wellbeing. In most cases, the real need is for encouragement, support, knowledge and skills.

This is what Life Surfing offers.

We have developed a range of services – one-to-one coaching, training workshops, mentoring groups and a range of publications - to give you the knowledge, skills and motivation needed to address life's issues and overcome stress-related problems in a healthy way, and to promote your long-term personal wellbeing.

For further information, please visit the Life Surfing website:

www.life-surfing.com
info@life-surfing.com

Or you can contact us on: 0300 321 4514 / 07922 537 646

Life Surfing
Box 124, R&R Consulting Centre
41 St. Isan Road
Heath
Cardiff CF14 4LW

Life Surfing is a community interest company limited by guarantee
(07399335) registered in England and Wales